First Flight

AF228652

Contents

written by John Lockyer

Years ago, people watched birds fly
and wished that they could fly, too.

2

Some people tried to fly using kites, gliders, and balloons. These flying machines had no power. They needed the wind to stay up in the air.

Orville and Wilbur Wright lived in the United States. They were both interested in flying. They built large gliders with strong, light materials.

They tied strings to the gliders'
wings and flew them like kites. Then
they pulled the strings to keep the
wings straight. The gliders helped
them learn how air moves.

One glider was big enough to carry
a person. Wilbur flew in it for ten
seconds. He found out how to keep
the glider level in the air.

The two brothers built many flying machines. One machine had an engine, control levers, two wings, and two propellers. They called it the Flyer.

In 1903, the Wright brothers took the Flyer to the sand dunes near Kitty Hawk in North Carolina. The Flyer was put on long rails on top of the sand.

Orville and Wilbur tossed a coin to see which one would be the first pilot. Orville won. He had to lie down on the bottom wing between the two propellers.

The Flyer rolled slowly down the rails.
Orville used his hands and his hips
to work the control levers. He didn't
have a crash helmet or a safety belt!

The wind was strong, so Wilbur ran beside the Flyer. He held onto the wing to stop it from dropping into the sand.

Lift-off! The Flyer wobbled, but it stayed in the air for 12 seconds! Orville had made the world's first powered flight.

Orville and Wilbur made four more flights on that special day. The longest time the Flyer stayed in the air was 59 seconds.

The Wright brothers built more planes. They learned how to turn them in the air. They also learned how to land safely. Soon they could fly for as long as an hour.

Then they built a plane with a seat for a passenger as well as the pilot. Now people fly all over the world!